LIGHT REAI

Light Reading

Stephan Delbos

BLAZEVOX[BOOKS]
Buffalo, New York

Light Reading
by Stephan Delbos

Published by BlazeVOX [books]

Printed in the United States of America

Interior design and typesetting by Geoffrey Gatza
Cover Art: Josef Sudek
Svàty Vit, 1928
Photograph © 2018 Museum of Fine Arts, Boston.

First Edition
ISBN: 978-1-60964-320-1
Library of Congress Control Number: 2018951452

BlazeVOX [books]
131 Euclid Ave
Kenmore, NY 14217
Editor@blazevox.org

publisher of weird little books

BlazeVOX [books]

blazevox.org

21 20 19 18 17 16 15 14 13 12 01 02 03 04 05 06 07 08 09 10

BlazeVOX

Contents:

LIGHT READING

I: Light Reading

what you cried when you came from the womb is your name

§Aubade

(shakes speaker)

§Poet

and just like that
I was wearing Johnnie Walker's hat

§Last Night (Tone Loathing)

dirty
angular
face

§Lust

she said I won't
forget you it
sounded like a threat

§Late Sooth

a hole with a

hole in it

she wrote

a kind
of toast

to
mourning

§Wrought Light

cannot believe I have lived
here so long

§Earth Forty

keytar & flowbee see
anything can be poetry

§'80s Ars

if only
all life
were so
simple
here
hang
your
shells
shadows
shame

§On Coatracks

shapely

breaks

easily

§Umbrella Lines

I think I
will still
try
to survive

Darkness
-’s static
soundtracks me

§Twenty-first Century Man

impossibly

yes

§Luck

if I could meddle
in moss
between cobblestones
tamped by footprints
& sunlight or be
a samurai I'd don
the latter's armor
honoring neither
choice nor indecision
simply cutting
any matter
in my way

§After Ovid

grim daguerreotype
mugshot leers
from early age
        a distant
            avant
-                garde

I'd like to meet the man
who tailored his dust
            jacket such
sharp

cuts

§Маяковский In Translation

dappled doppelgänger

of my Latin teacher

§Sweet Jesuít

paper windows

typewriting rain

light claws tornado

I find myself think

funny naming storms

§William Bronk

if I myself am hell
& hell is other people
I is another

§Bibliography

grasssnake—

§Mount Holyoke

get out

yr gun

we done

come

full

circ

-le

wine

jugular

§Kerouac In Florida

these are only notes for after intermission

§Alexandrine

Fedoras eating Egg Foo Young
At 2 o'clock in the morning

§New York City In The Old Days

xx

xxxx

lycanthropic thirst

§Full Moon Bender

the more I think

about dreaming

the more I dream

about thinking

§Yonkers

two teams
same scrum

§Election Day

crept to depth
this belief

explosions
splendid

mean freedom even

§4th of July

they came for me I was gone

§Fight/Flight

favorite architectural affectation

sgraffito

say it

like Rico

Suave

§Unbidden Tour

heat   licks

foot   prints

from

wood

§Sauna

water bridges

bridges

§Fifty-Year Flood

what poems
are stuck
in there

§Passing Towns By Train

I wouldn’t piss on his shadow

§Binary Respect

undisguised
disgust

§Gin The First Time

eventually Middle East
of what one wonders
o Copernicus

§Accidental Occident

;

§Broken Wing

without my words

your words

are uh
alone

you know

§Title's Entitlement

write   yr name
means   tattoo
little   toenail
backward angel

Benjamin's
history dragged
wreckage never
icarused

gargantuan
wings flapt
wind gnawed
fist not

this
whispered
Walter

away

§Signature In Quotation Marks

ACTUALLY

AUSCHWITZ

AFTER POETRY

IS BARBARIC

§Daring Adorno

they made our names of words

§Why Writing

e v e n i n g

for a reason

pale perfect handoff

day | night sliced

horizon dark | light

crooked coast

we could see our parents

' house touch point years

solstice

balance

soul | cool mortal
coil

§Brothers Midsummer

flocks of song outside

we drop the glasses   words
are to bear

breakable parts for   stranger
fingers as air

& light   enfold
untouchable   birds

§Rosy-Fingered Dawn

I’m only
here for the plum
wine

§Chinese Restaurant Playboy

microphone in headlights

§Poem

wand-
ering

with
cider

glass type

-writer

§Autumn Prague

2 Vietnamese
waitresses melt
in silky smoky Smíchov night

§Bohemian Noir

in tiny pieces
tiny parts

i whose
bruises

broke pillows

sleep under
paper sheets

§Fragments (Keepsake)

for what

we have

made of what

we are

§Thanksgiving

look out the hollow of the body that holds you

§Mehr Licht Lullaby

II: Bagatelles for Typewriter

BAGATELLE FOR VÁCLAV HAVEL, CIMBALOM & HOARSE KAZOO

Wicked fingers of time conspire on clocks to pinch us

by soul-scruff

buds of Petřín's sleeping apples

and pears thrum in arpeggios of snowflakes

a black swath

falls off the roof

of Prague's National Theatre

O Coca Cola

decals on Café Slavia windows

o irony immortal

put on a play we are ready to laugh so deep

we vomit every word

for fear of censure revolution like

Darwin said it hurts

//// I am swinging on a velvet swing

I am standing

on a sidewalk loitering inside the afternoon

of fractured urban chorus gum chewers

prostheltyzing cacophany

I am thinking of you

Václav Havel

the gavel fell on your

pencil forcing

intermission

Mr. President

in Little Buddha Bistro   you sat

at the next table   eating

spring rolls years ago

In your favorite café   Slavia the day after

you died   I drank coffee

No one noticed

my Lowellian

sorrow my black jacket

Sněženky thumb through Petřín's mud

subterranean

s
p
i
r
e
s

you have been three months among ////////// At Strahov Monastery you are out

of the ordinary   So too at Letná

where I watch

a man conduct the dance

of Saint Vitus   music of the fears

feeling of the beers

and over on Gogolova   a window shuttered shatters
expectation

men in high boxes

swivel enormous cranes   Life is porno

scrawled on a rusty streetlamp
Bird's nests   something

I'd forgotten   hatch

in spindled branches   Elsewhere

Bacchus Is Among Us

scratched on a column in a courtyard

peopled with detached statues

This was yours

too

////////////////////////// Evening in Žižkov where Seifert the poet was born

and you dug underground

withyourtunnelgun

typewriter and a deep

desk
drawer

What history lay in store

for your ampersand monologues against

shop window propaganda

Wearing the rusty headgear of a hangover I walk Havelian

by crumbling smokestacks of Smíchov   everywhere

in this backstage city

hoisting cables

irony insight naive love

his   syllables   lift   us

BAGATELLE FOR PRAGUE, PLYMOUTH & MEMORY STICK

At Strahov

I stop

ears cocked

to
a window where air rushes
at me

puckered with sound
a garage
band's not altogether
terrible Anarchy in the UK

There are
many ways to get what you want

so I ramble

around

the ruined stadium

down

by my old dormitory

dreaming
of a letter
that's waited

the quarter-score years I've lived elsewhere

it lies
in the back

of a pigeonhole
no longer named for me
lobby
where I do not exist
Something is written
there

one word

that will change my l i f e

The story of this journey starts

here s u n b u r n Mom said
ruthless

signifier

Skin sloughed in childhood sand dunes

Long howl down corridors
of air to this threshold city where ocean

is literary creation and

I carry music like Samson

in my beard and later

on my Samsung

listen
something wonderful has happened

to all of us here we are

BAGATELLE FOR TU FU, SZECHUAN TOFU, TSING TAO, LI PO & PLATE SPINNER

April shows a nipple but only one. For five days

I have sold my waking hours. A fool, like the cook

who walks ranting from the closet kitchen with plates

shaped like frisbees long slow prayer of spring

park afternoon, perfect toss unlabored, hovering

may not deign to sink unlike my plate

of tofu, rehydrated mushrooms, yellow peppers,

ginger slop and rice; half-drunken lunch. Never

was I so alone. Such lunch! Tu Fu's buddy Li Po

died trying to hug the moon with sodden arms

reflected in a river. In my mind sometimes I am

in China, falling through the Chinese air,

pockets filled with teriyaki chicken wings. I live

a six-month journey from my parents, wear

their ages, a grandfather clock earring. Pain.

What the T'ang poets took for granted: language

outlives us. The waitress asks do you want chopsticks?

Of course but rice is difficultly singular so I lick

surreptitiously the plate when she goes. Spicy

moon.

BAGATELLE FOR ANCIENT VALUES, JAW HARP & LYRE

What is worth believing
is impossible

to believe and really only
that will save you
someday from pyres
of doubt
sorrow
deprivation

Ghost notes
don't know they are
not there
phantom limbs
irrefutable evidence
of forces injurious
conspiring
to deprive us of ourselves
and one another
Don't do this Odysseus

screamed the suitors

The mystery unites us
or shall we
recognize the microchip
the matchbook
the God particle catalytic
convertors
snowblowers
sea bream fillet shucked oysters
instant coffee
windowsill orchids
personal computers
personal space

social media

space heaters
take-out Styrofoam first-class
Grammy nominations
soft drinks shampoo
plus conditioner
in one dandruff
eczema flatulence
not the stuff I assure you myths
are made of

There be dragons

BAGATELLE FOR GYÖRGI LIGETI, ETERNAL LIGHT & HONEYCOMB

Swim in the swarm
of voices
vices of silence
Lux Aeterna
air
colored with tears
not yet
battered by swallowing
ground Keep
listening
cvcn flame makes a sound
Outside among enormous ashes
trees wind sifts
and microchips in digital
cameras register
the phenomena   This
too is Lux Aeterna
Shut your eyes

your brain a beehive
honey tastes like blood

Eternity another way
to say thank you
but not just yet
Even our organs outlive us
if only briefly
and when we really feel
life we say
struck a chord
So clarify
emotion lives
in ears and eyes
like oysters harboring hoarding
pearls

Every chapel
echo-chamber
echo-chamber
when we call for silence
we only want
the single sound
foghorn or boatman's call

BAGATELLE FOR PHILIP GLASS & PIPE ORGAN IN LIEU OF PRAYER

Thoughtless on a sunny day | empowered by the radiance | let us pray

forgive the merciless | indifference we pay | tabernacle

and tackle box | how easy tiny joys | elude us

Joy eludes us | yet we | preening | pride

in the annihilated need | to kneel before anything | unless observing

ceremonies necessary | to get ahead | to heaven or the boardroom

\

As an altar boy I loved | velvet silences of sacristies

brass taper-holders | bell-shaped snuff that flamed a hand

to reach me as I | mischievous | melted old wax

with a wooden match | hollered | in my head the Devil

I felt had found me | a moment before | returning to

the grim serenity of God

BAGATELLE FOR DOUBT & WIND INSTRUMENTS

I am listening to music
less than listless
Outside deaf snow baffles
edges of every open object
and if O glorious
if I were nay scotchsick
almost I would dance
in my mind out in it
only thinking of myself
and the maniacal warmth
of this room built
for living
A prayer is what
we say when we
cannot be sure
A dumb song

No yes no
yes no yes
as when one sees
an erstwhile lover
the moment of a nosebleed
Who needs that
Oh you I do
not know what you might be
looking for but my heart
hurts this white February

morning when books will not
speak to me
and words are not real
enough or deep
you see
Hear me
narrow fellow

in this fallow silence

BAGATELLE FOR THROAT SINGERS, BATON & PLAYER PIANO

I am a terrible Buddhist
my love you are a magnificent adversary
on the anniversary of
our first nervous kiss a sidewalk where
garbage cans held fish
-bones, failed ficuses, Orangina bottles,
our alcohol the pilot
light of love; this was supposed to be
about enlightenment,
the impossible tightrope possibility.
Thinking about nothing
in particular I ripped my underwear.
Wow, how terrific
I might have said if I owned another
pair the dainty blue
of Danube. Outside Vltava interminable
O city, old riversong
scared of dying and so forth like erstwhile
composers who knew
how to wear the hell out of a pince-nez.
None of that is over now.

BAGATELLE FOR TORNADO, SELF-INFLICTED GUNSHOT, CHOPIN'S FINGERNAIL CLIPPER, SINCERITY & JEST

The kindest words bitterest music

We cannot define the line we must not cross to save the hero ourself from loss

and guttural regret

Et cetera until the silent end Look out! Behind you!

In the basement we kept trophies and my father's guns plus a case of sterilized

water preparation for eventualities concerning thirst

and the apocalypse

Will I ever have a basement and a case for items just in case

Sympathy of a symphony will the deaf never know you

And the gluttony of savings forever to be withheld from me

A fate worse than faith There it is! In front of you!

III: Arrangements

<I>

1. A poem in terza rima
2. A poem of 18 lines
3. A poem containing the phrase coin slot
4. A poem rhyming beguile and tinfoil
5. A poem with two mirrored meanings
6. A poem under the sign of Scorpio
7. A poem undertaken in November
8. A poem that knows it is a poem
9. A poem titled “Apostrophe”
10. A poem that never asked to be born

<II>

1. A poem with a chessed past
2. A poem set to Sibelius
3. A poem of 30 years silence
4. A constipated poem
5. A poem entitled “Possible Monogamy”
6. A poem never to be heard
7. An hermetic poem
8. A poem of ten lines and ten syllables
9. A new villanelle
10. A poem double-crossed

<III>

1. Another form called "Short Order"
2. A poem with one noun
3. A poem with six verbs
4. A poem with three adverbs
5. A poem with one dark adjective
6. A poem with one missing piece
7. A parquet jigsaw
8. Childhood sleepovers and Micro Machines
9. A poem quick like an auctioneer
10. A poem as the crow flies

<IV>

1. A poem controlled by someone else
2. A someone who doesn't speak your language
3. A poem with two tongues
4. An indiscrete poem
5. A champagne bottle buried under Atlantic
6. Skyscraper built on a schooner
7. A mudskipper
8. The Chicago Black Sox
9. A poem excluding the word "the"
10. A poem another alphabet

<V>

1. A poem in bio-waste bag font
2. A poem holding its breath
3. A one-lung poem
4. A poem that cannot hear itself think
5. A poem getting on my last nerve
6. A poem huffing oxygen
7. A poem title is the last line
8.
9. A poem with seven monorhymed lines
10. A poem curing emphysema

<VI>

1. An unremarkable poem
2. A sonnet with three voltas
3. In each line
4. A poem folded on itself
5. The poem ate a data processor
6. A poem rhyming “processor” with “blackout”
7. A poem with diplomatic immunity
8. A poem Ovid would have scoffed
9. A poem drunk on wordscotch
10. The pebble in hopscotch

<VII>

1. A poem human highlight film
2. A 21-line salute
3. A poem in Atlanta Georgia
4. Tape for the knuckle line
5. Breaks a poem with enjambed thumb
6. A poem for Dominique Wilkins
7. A poem with a tight fade
8. A poem on the court
9. reverse in written poem A
10. Poem with a pump fake

<VIII>

1. A poem in CAPS LOCK
2. A loudmouth poem
3. A poem eating pickled eggs
4. A giggly poem tehehe
5. A poem of unknown vintage
6. A poem with a thinking problem
7. Sign here x________________
8. A poem shakey shakey
9. A poem with nothing left to do
10. A poem that does not need you

<IX>

1. A poem first word each line rhymed
2. A poem each line ends with “a”
3. Poem in memory of Nintendo
4. A poem with a Power Glove
5. A poem for *Nintendo Power* magazine
6. Master Blaster poem
7. A poem with infinite lives
8. Up up down down left right left right B A B A start
9. A poem contra sunlight
10. A poem you have to blow on

<X>

1. A poem on a dryer sheet
2. A poem with static cling
3. A poem stuck to that first May
4. A poem losing its virginity
5. Pediddle poem a punch buggy
6. A poem that could save any Amy
7. A poem that hasn't read *Ulysses*
8. A poem that hates talking
9. This is and isn't the end of the poem
10. A poem with too many doors

NOTES

Light Reading

"Маяковский In Translation": Vladimir Mayakovsky (1893–1930) was an innovative Russian poet.

"Sweet Jesuít": Gerard Manley Hopkins (1844–1889) was an innovative English poet and Jesuit priest. His poem "Pied Beauty" begins with the line: "Glory be to God for dappled things –."

"William Bronk": William Bronk (1918–1999) was an American poet.

"Bibliography": "I myself am hell" is Robert Lowell's paraphrase of Satan from Milton's *Paradise Lost* (1667) in his poem "Skunk Hour" from *Life Studies* (1959). "Hell is other people" comes from Jean-Paul Sartre's play *No Exit* (1944). "I is another" comes from Rimbaud in 1871.

"Mount Holyoke": Emily Dickinson (1830–1886) went to Mount Holyoke College and later wrote the poem "A narrow Fellow in the Grass" about a snake which is also referenced in this book in the poem "Bagatelle for Doubt & Wind Instruments."

"Kerouac in Florida": The American writer Jack Kerouac (1922–1969) spent his last years in Florida, where he died of complications due to alcoholism.

"New York City In The Old Days": Egg Foo Young is a Chinese-American dish. It was popular in the United States in the 1930s.

"Unbidden Tour": Sgraffito is a technique for decorating walls and facades with contrasting colors, most often black and white. It is common in Central European cities, including Prague.

"Accidental Occident": Copernicus (1473–1543) was an astronomer who proposed a model of the universe centered around the Sun rather than the Earth.

"Signature in Quotation Marks": In his essay "On the Concept of History" (1940), German Jewish philosopher and cultural critic Walter Benjamin (1892–1940) envisioned the angel of history, citing Paul Klee's painting *Angelus Novus* (1920), thus: "His face is turned toward the past. Where we perceive a chain of events, he sees one single catastrophe which keeps piling wreckage and hurls it in front of his feet. The angel would like to stay, awaken the dead, and make whole what has been smashed. But a storm is blowing in from Paradise; it has got caught in his wings with such a violence that the angel can no longer close them. The storm irresistibly propels him into the future to which his back is turned, while the pile of debris before him grows skyward. This storm is what we call progress." See: *Illuminations*, trans. Harry Zohn, New York: Schocken Books, 1969: 249. Benjamin committed suicide in Portbou, Spain while fleeing the Third Reich.

"Daring Adorno": In his 1949 essay "Cultural Criticism and Society," cultural theorist Theodore Adorno (1903–1969) wrote: "To write poetry after Auschwitz is barbaric."

"Rosy-Fingered Dawn": The phrase "rosy-fingered Dawn" appears several times in English translations of *The Odyssey* and *The Iliad.*

"Bohemian Noir": Smíchov is a working-class district in Prague, where several Vietnamese families own Chinese restaurants.

"Mehr Licht Lullaby": "Mehr licht," German for "more light," were the last words of German poet and Renaissance man Johann Wolfgang von Goethe (1749–1832).

Bagatelles for Typewriter

A bagatelle is a French term meaning a trifle. It is most often associated with short classical music compositions.

"Bagatelle for Václav Havel, Cimbalom & Hoarse Kazoo": Václav Havel (1936–2011) was a playwright and the President of Czechoslovakia and later the Czech Republic. His book *Anticodes* (1964) is a collection of concrete poems. The cimbalom is an instrument often played in Czech folk music. "Sněženky" are flowers known in English as Galanthus or Snowdrop. All of the streets and places named in the poem are in Prague. "Coca Cola decals" refers to the controversial reconstruction of Prague's Café Slavia, a place frequented by intellectuals since its opening in 1884. "Lowellian sorrow" refers to the American poet Robert Lowell, who wrote elegies for several political figures. Lowell's poem "Election Night," which appears directly after the poem "From Prague 1968" in his collection *History* (1973), includes the lines: "today I wore my blue knitted tie to class. / No one understood that blue meant black…." Jaroslav Seifert (1901–1986) was a Czech poet and winner of the Nobel Prize.

"Bagatelle for Prague, Plymouth & Memory Stick": "Many ways to get what you want" is a line from the Sex Pistols song "Anarchy in the UK." (1977) In *The Winter's Tale* (1611) Shakespeare describes Bohemia as "a desert country near the sea."

"Bagatelle for Tu Fu, Szechuan Tofu, Tsing Tao, Li Po & Plate Spinner": Tu Fu (712 AD–770 AD) and Li Po (701 AD–762 AD) were friends and fellow poets in the T'ang Dynasty, China. They are considered the greatest poets of the Golden Age of Chinese poetry. Szechuan Tofu is a spicy tofu dish. Tsing Tao is a Chinese beer. Plate spinning, an acrobatic performance in which a person dexterously spins plates, bowls and other flat objects on poles, originated in ancient China.

"Bagatelle for Ancient Values, Jaw Harp & Lyre": According to Samson in the King James Bible: "with the jawbone of an ass, heaps upon heaps, with the jaw of an ass have I slain a thousand men" (Judges 15:16). A jaw harp is a hand-held instrument favored by hobos and beggars. In ancient Greek society, hubris was punishable and hospitality was a virtue. Odysseus came home disguised as a beggar and killed all the suitors taking advantage of his wife's hospitality.

"Bagatelle for György Ligeti, Eternal Light & Honeycomb": György Sándor Ligeti (1923–2006) was an avant-garde Hungarian-Austrian composer.

“Bagatelle for Philip Glass & Pipe Organ in Lieu of Prayer”: American composer Philip Glass, whose album *Glassworks* (1982) influenced this poem, performed at Archa Theatre in Prague on November 9, 2016.

“Bagatelle for Throat Singers, Baton & Player Piano”: The Vltava River runs through Prague. Like the Elbe and the Danube, the Vltava is known by several names and has been featured in classical music as well as literature. “An der schönen blauen Donau,” or “By the Beautiful Blue Danube,” is a waltz Johann Strauss II (1825–1899) composed in 1866. Pince-nez is a style of glasses that pinch your nose rather than rest behind your ear. Most men of achievement in the 19th century wore them at one time or another.

“Bagatelle for Tornado, Self-inflicted Gunshot, Chopin’s Fingernail Clipper, Sincerity & Jest”: Frédéric François Chopin (1810–1849) was a Polish composer and virtuoso pianist of the Romantic era.

Arrangements

“<II>”: Jean Sibelius (1865–1957) was a Finnish classical composer who stopped composing at the height of his powers and produced virtually no music during the last 30 years of his life.

“<III>”: Micro Machines were very small cars that were popular children’s toys in the 1990s. The commercials were narrated by John Moschitta Jr., a fast-talking spokesperson.

“<VII>”: Dominique Wilkins was an NBA player, number 21 with the Atlanta Hawks from 1982 until 1994. He won two NBA Slam Dunk Contests, in 1985 and 1990. In 1986 he was the NBA Scoring Champion. One of his signature dunks was a reverse pump fake.

“<IX>”: Nintendo is a popular video game entertainment system. *Nintendo Power* was a gaming magazine that ran from 1991 until 2012. The Power Glove was a Nintendo accessory. The code in line eight is for infinite lives in the game *Contra* (1988). As anyone who ever owned Nintendo knows, you had to blow on the game cartridges to get them to work, because dust and other particulate matter would get stuck on the contact points. Every gamer had his or her own elaborate series of maneuvers to get a game functioning again.

“<X>”: Pediddle and punch buggy are full-contact sports played aggressively by siblings and suggestively by lovers in cars up and down the East Coast.

Acknowledgements

Sincere thanks to the editors of *SAND*, *Molly Bloom* and *VLAK*, and the curators of Prague's ArtSPACE Gallery at Anglo-American University, where versions of some of these poems appeared.

To Amy, Theodore, Julian: you have called me to the dance. To my mother, father and brothers, 13/1620 forever. To Christopher Crawford, Joshua Mensch, Michael Stein, Jan Zikmund, Justin Quinn, Benjamin Cunningham, Philip Heijmans, Ken Nash, Scott Nixon, Nathan Fields, Damien Galeone, Mark Terrill, Cralan Kelder, Max Munson, Douglas Shields Dix, Louis Armand, Chard deNiord, Burt Kimmelman, Norman Finkelstein, Michael Waters, Joshua Weiner, Chris Fahey, Chris Ackley, Elizabeth Gross, Seth Rogoff, Padraic Dugan, Kevin Touhey, Tony Ozuna, Tony Marais, Zuzana Volmuthová and Gil Fleischman, it's working.

Stephan Delbos is a writer living in Prague. His poetry, essays and translations have been published internationally. He is the editor of *From a Terrace in Prague: A Prague Poetry Anthology* (Litteraria Pragensia, 2011). His play *Chetty's Lullaby*, about trumpet player Chet Baker, was produced in San Francisco in 2014. His co-translation of *The Absolute Gravedigger*, by Czech surrealist poet Vítězslav Nezval, was awarded the PEN/Heim Translation Grant in 2015 and was published by Twisted Spoon Press in 2016. *Deaf Empire*, his play about Czech composer Bedřich Smetana, was produced by the Prague Shakespeare Company in 2017. He is the author of the poetry chapbook *In Memory of Fire* (Cape Cod Poetry Review, 2017), and the poetry collection *Small Talk* (Literární Salon, 2019). A Founding Editor of the web journal *B O D Y*, he teaches at Charles University and Anglo-American University in Prague.

Made in the USA
Middletown, DE
14 June 2021

42210315R00061